YOU MAY NOT NEED A LAWYER

WHY EVERY CASE DOES NOT NEED A LAWYER AND WHAT YOU CAN DO ABOUT IT

Christopher Washington

Disclaimer

All knowledge contained in this book is given for informational and educational purposes only. This book does not replace the need to consult an attorney when the situation calls for expert legal advice. The author is not in any way accountable for any results or outcomes that emanate from using this material. Constructive attempts have been made to provide information that is both accurate and effective, but the author is not bound for the accuracy or use/misuse of this information.

Table of Contents

INTRODUCTION

This book is based on the principles of personal injury law and the foundations that must be understood in order to obtain a fair and just resolution. Personal injury law refers to situations where someone suffers injury, loss or damages due to the negligence or omission of another individual or corporation. The purpose of this body of law is to compensate the injured party or restore them as much as possible to the position they held before the injury. The purpose and intent of Personal injury laws are to compensate the plaintiff (injured or harmed person) for whatever injuries and losses he/she suffers as a result of the actions or inactions of the defendant (person who caused the injury or loss). The responsible person, corporation, and/or his insurance is expected restore the injured party. Personal injury compensation is expected to restore the value of what was lost or taken; not award money arbitrarily without rhyme or reason.

Personal injury law can be very complex and complicated, however, there are still situations where you do not necessarily need the services of a lawyer.

This book attempts to provide guidance in these situations and the proper procedures for the handling of a personal injury claim. It gives the guidelines for knowing when it becomes necessary to engage a lawyer as well as tips on choosing a competent lawyer.

CHAPTER ONE

SELF-SETTLEMENT

You may have become accustomed to the mentality that **ALL** legal disputes, losses, or injuries require the involvement of a lawyer. Most people share this belief, and there can be significant problems for failure to engage the services of a lawyer when legal expertise is truly needed.

However, there are a limited amount of injuries, losses, or complexities in some of these disputes that allow them to be settled with or without the services of a lawyer.

Property Damage

Minor Property damage refers to the damage done to the objects and property of an individual after a minor automobile accident. This category mainly consists of minor collisions that occur in parking lots, private driveways, and public roadways where either there is no damage, the damage is limited to paint transfer, or the property damage estimates are less than $500.00. At the outset of an accident, property damage claims should be filed immediately. The responsible insurance company usually responds promptly when the damage is minor and there is little to no dispute over the value of the damage. After any damage to property, it is recommended that you contact your insurance company as well as the insurance company of the defendant, and setup a claim with the insurance companies. A lawyer is not needed to set up the claim, however, if retained, the lawyer usually takes care of this step for the client. Nevertheless, in the case where the insurance company is unwilling to pay or only willing to pay a value less than what's fair and reasonable, the assistance of a lawyer becomes necessary. If your vehicle is a total loss, you should verify the value of the vehicle on kbb.com. If your vehicle is not a total loss and repair to a good working condition is an option, you should get an estimate from 1-2 auto repair shops. DO NOT rely solely on the property damage estimate provided by the insurance company's property damage adjuster that comes out to look at your car. Oftentimes, there is hidden damage that only becomes noticeable once a reputable repair shop does a thorough inspection of your vehicle. The insurance company adjuster usually does a very limited inspection, which routinely misses more significant issues.

Minor Injuries

Many people are involved in car accidents, falls, and other personal injuries daily due to negligence or carelessness of others. The gravity and severity of such injuries and losses are a factor to consider in your decision whether to hire a lawyer or not.

If you truly have a minor injury with little or no medical treatment, you can negotiate a reasonable settlement with the party at fault or his insurance company, so the services of a lawyer would not be essential in the settlement.

For example, in a case where there is an ER visit and no other treatment or an ER visit with 3 or fewer follow-ups with a health care provider, it's reasonable to settle the case without a lawyer.

In fact, the net settlement (actual dollar amount client puts in their pocket) in such situations might be equal to or slightly more than the net amount that would be received if a lawyer is involved.

Caveat: Minor property damage does not automatically mean minor injury. Thousands of people are seriously injured and killed annually when they are involved in accidents with minor property damage.

WARNING: The above options to resolve your claim without a lawyer comes with the following warnings:

1. Oftentimes, the severity of injuries, damages, and losses is not fully known for several weeks and oftentimes months-so one should be very careful and cautious before accepting a rushed settlement.

2. Health Care Providers have the right to be paid for services they provided, and the insurance company may settle with you while neglecting the health care providers you owe as a result of injuries sustained in

the accident. This could result in a lawsuit or collection attempts by the health care provider and damage to your credit.

3. Private Health Insurance Providers, Medicaid, and Medicare have a right to be reimbursed for any payments they made on your behalf. This is a highly technical body of law and ignoring the reimbursement rights of these entities could subject you to a lawsuit and adversely affect your benefits.

It Demands A Lawyer

If you have been involved in an accident that you initially thought was minor but any of the conditions or situations discussed below arise, it is recommended that you contact a lawyer.

If you have been involved in an accident and any of the following is present, consulting a lawyer is recommended and significantly improves the likelihood of you being fully compensated for your injuries, harms, and losses:

1. Headaches, Neck, or back injuries that are constant and daily

2. Diagnostic test (x-ray,MRI, CT Scans, etc.) reveal that you have structural damage to any body part.

3. TBI (Traumatic Brain Injury) symptoms include but are not limited to:

SYMPTOMS OF TBI

Appears dazed or stunned
Answers questions slowly
Nausea or vomiting
Sensitivity to light
Impaired memory of events prior to wreck
Headache

Nausea
Vomiting
Dizziness
Fatigue
Blurred vision
Sleep disturbance
Sensitivity to light/noise
Balance problems
Transient neurological abnormalities
Reduced attention
Memory complaints
Reduced speed of processing
Impaired judgment
Impaired executive function

Increased irritability
Social withdrawal
Increased frustration
Depression

4. Psychological Injuries

5. Permanent Scars

6. Injury to any other body part that is unresolved and does not appear that it will be fully resolved within the first 30 days following the accident.

The opinions and expertise of a lawyer are recommended in these situations because it is not easy to predict the settlement value of such an injury, especially the lifelong value of the injury. A trained lawyer will research prior cases to find the appropriate value, as well as hire experts in the medical field, and financial fields, such as accounting or economics, to pinpoint the appropriate value.

The decision to contact a lawyer should be executed the very moment you realize you have a problem that is unlikely to be completely resolved in the next 30 days. As a final note, personal injury cases are usually handled on a contingency fee basis, which means the lawyer advances all costs associated with the case and the client has no up-front cost, so please do not allow a limited ability or absolute non-ability to hire a lawyer to delay your contacting one if you have determined that one is needed for your case.

CHAPTER TWO

SETTING UP CLAIM

Setting up a claim is the process of letting the insurance company or companies know that you were involved in an accident and suffered an injury or loss.

You might find the procedure for setting up a claim complicated and cumbersome if you have never filed a personal injury claim, and this chapter aims to eradicate the complexities that may be faced by a first timer. It is also to ensure mistakes are not made even for people that have filed them once or twice. Be prepared to answer questions concerning the following:

1. Biographical Information of the parties
   a. Name
   b. Address
   c. DOB

d. Phone Number

e. Etc.

2. Injuries sustained and any related medical treatment

3. The location of the accident.

4. The date of the accident.

5. A statement concerning how the accident occurred

   a. Note: In 99% of our cases we refuse to allow our client to give a recorded statement to the defendant's insurance company discussing how the accident occurred or going into details concerning injuries.

   b. However, you may be required to give a recorded statement to your own insurance company. Please review the policy or contact a lawyer for help.

6. Photographs and videos that were taken of the accident scene and the vehicles or other objects involved.

7. Is there a police report?

8. Everything that happened leading up to, during, and after the accident

9. The name and contact information concerning witnesses

10. Property Damage including, the extent of the damage and the location of any damaged property, so that the insurance company can have an investigator or adjuster take a look at it.

CHAPTER THREE

Insurance Adjusters

This specific category of people is referred to differently by different people. Claims adjuster, claims handler, and insurance adjuster all refer to the same category of people who function in the same role.

An insurance adjuster refers to an individual who acts as a middleman between the insured, the injured party, and the insurance company in determining the amount of money that should be paid to resolve a claim. Oftentimes, the insurance company assigns a different adjuster for your property damage and bodily injury claims.

Insurance adjusters determine the value of your claim thorough investigation and evaluation. The adjusters conduct their investigation and evaluation by reviewing the following:

1. Statements of the parties and witnesses
2. Photographs of the scene and vehicles/objects involved
3. Review police reports
4. Review of case law
5. Review of medical records and bills

    a. Be careful about signing blank medical releases that allow insurance companies to retrieve your records. There's no way for you to know exactly what they have requested.

    b. A better practice is for you to obtain a copy of all the relevant records and bills and forward them to the insurance company.

6. Review claims databases to see if you have prior claim(s)

    a. Insurance companies have a database that they share with each other. This allows them to search for all prior claims you may have made.

CHAPTER FOUR

PITFALLS

There are some significant errors that people can make while trying to handle their personal injury case without the assistance of a lawyer. These errors can have significant and permanent adverse effect on the overall outcome of a case.

Oftentimes, a google search and review of articles and a few lawyers' websites is insufficient education to allow one to handle a personal injury case with complex issues. Having acquired some basic knowledge about the topic, it is possible that you may enter settlement negotiation or resolution of your case while overlooking significant compensation that you may be entitled to.

The following are some of the mistakes made concerning personal injury law:

Settling your claim at the scene of the accident. It is impossible to know the extent of your injuries at this point in time. Furthermore, in most personal injury cases you have one year to file a lawsuit before your case prescribes "**or dies**", so there should be no rush.

Delay in seeking medical treatment

After an accident, you should get a medical checkup to determine if you have been injured. Additionally, many people feel fine immediately after an accident and start having pain and discomfort in the days and weeks that follow. You should get any and all medical treatment recommended by your doctors as soon as practically possible.

Providing statements that can be misinterpreted: telling the insurance company there were no injuries, or you feel fine often causes them to deny or undervalue your claim if you later report injuries.

Settling your claim while battling medical problems. Oftentimes, people just wish to put the entire incident behind them and will resolve their claim even though they are still receiving medical treatment and their long-term prognosis is unknown. This is a very bad idea. Once you settle your case, you cannot come back later no matter how bad your injuries or losses are.

CHAPTER FIVE

<u>PROPERTY DAMAGE</u>

Property damage refers to the damage, loss or destruction to property. This entails damage to any property--including property such as cell phones or eyeglasses that can be damaged while inside an automobile involved in an accident.

Property damage claims require proof similar to bodily injury claims. In most situations, the property damage claim is resolved fairly quickly and in fact, the insurance company is required to make a payment within 30 days of satisfactory proof of loss. Compensation available for damage or loss of your property includes:

1. The value of the loss or damage if the property is totally destroyed or loss

2. The loss of use of your property for any time period, if it is repairable

3. A decrease in the value of the property if it is worth less after being repaired.

The insurance company will require proof of the property damage and the best way to obtain that proof and maximize your recovery is to:

1. Take pictures of the damage to your car
2. Bring your car to 1-2 repair shops for estimates; it's also advisable to request the repair shop take pictures
3. Share all your evidence with the insurance company
4. Review the blue book value of your vehicle on kbb.com to compare it with the figures the insurance company presents to you to resolve your claim.
5. Lastly, the insurance company will send out a property damage adjuster to conduct an exam of your car. Warning: The figure he provides often is less than the

bluebook value or the figures your repair estimates may suggest. If the insurance company refuses to work with you to reach a fair resolution, it's advisable to seek the assistance of an attorney.

CHAPTER SIX

<u>MEDICAL BILLS</u>

Although medical treatment isn't required by law to substantiate a physical injury, claims adjusters will expect medical treatment to support your claim for injuries and will also request copies of your medical records and bills.

The defendant's insurance company will not pay your medical bills as they are incurred or become due but usually pay them as part of a lump sum amount when the case settles. Personal injury cases generally take between 6 months and 2 years to resolve. This can result in unpaid medical bills being sent to collections and adversely affecting your credit score. For this reason, it is advisable to submit medical bills to your health insurance provider or to your own liability insurance provider if you have purchased medical payments coverage as an additional add-on to your coverage. If your health insurance provider pays medical bills related to an accident they are entitled to reimbursement for those payments. However, there are situations where this reimbursement can be waived. Achieving this waiver, however, will most likely require the services of a personal injury attorney who also has experience resolving health insurance liens.

Medical Payments

Medical payments (med pay) refers to medical bills coverage only. The med pay refers to a concept or principle that is established to cover the payment of medical bills and treatment of injuries of individuals regardless of the party at fault. The coverage of med pay does not extend beyond medical bills directly related to injuries caused by auto accidents.

CHAPTER SEVEN

THE SETTLEMENT

PACKAGE

Up until this point, the term "settlement" has been mentioned repeatedly, without a thorough explanation of the concept and the content it truly entails. Thus, a settlement refers to the process of resolving the dispute that exists between parties. A settlement package, however, refers to the facts, details, and documents that contain the evidence of injury and losses caused by the accident.

A standard settlement package is expected to contain some definite documents that would aid the final decision while negotiating and settling a claim. These usually include the following:

1. Medical Records and bills-this provides the most definitive proof of your injuries and

the severity of them. You should include these documents in every settlement package. Failure to do so will result in the insurance company severely undervaluing your case.

2. Lost wages- apart from suffering physical injuries, an injured party can receive compensation for lost wages due to these injuries. In order to pay money for lost wages, the insurance company usually requires documentation from your employer showing time you missed following the accident as well as documentation in your medical records that excuse you from work for a period of time.

3. Property Damage- This is the simplest item of damages to resolve because it's simply math. Oftentimes, the property damage claim is settled prior to all other claims, however, if it is not resolved early on it should definitely be included in your settlement package.

4. Pain and Suffering- This refers to the physical, emotional, mental, and psychological pain and suffer that an individual endures. Absent legal training,

it's virtually impossible for a member of the public to determine a proper value for this claim. If you have significant pain and suffering that did not resolve within a few weeks, it's advisable to seek legal representation.

5. Loss of enjoyment of life-This refers to inability to do those things you enjoyed doing prior to the accident or a reduction in your ability and/or frequency in which you can do those things. Absent legal training, it's virtually impossible for a member of the public to determine a proper value for this claim. If you have significant loss of enjoyment of life problems that did not resolve within a few weeks, it's advisable to seek legal representation. It includes the following categories:

   a. Work activities
   b. Domestic activities
   c. Household activities
   d. Studies/educational activities
   e. Hobby activities
   f. Sports activities
   g. Traveling activities

h. Social activities

i. Activities with children

Secondly, organization is key in dealing with an insurance adjuster. You must ensure that your thoughts are organized through your conversations with an adjuster and also ensure that you note and organize the details and facts presented by the adjuster. This is important, so you will not accept an unfair offer, and it will be easier to proceed through the negotiation process.

Patience, It is essential you remain patient. Take careful notes while speaking to the adjuster and do not rush to accept the first offer they make. Take some time to review the adjuster's concerns and your notes and make a counter-offer that's centered on the severity of your injuries and the supporting documentation you've provided.

Whenever a settlement is finally reached, be sure to get the settlement agreement sent to you in writing. Remember, the adjuster has to pay you within 30 days of a settlement, however, this is contingent upon the settlement being in writing. Also, please remember that once your case is settled, you cannot come back for more later if you are still treating, if you have flair ups or if your condition deteriorates.

Below is a sample Format for a Settlement Letter:

<u>SETTLEMENT BRIEF OUTLINE</u>

INSIDE COVER PAGE (Appropriate title and photograph(s) or pages of photographs <u>of Plaintiff/Plaintiff's family</u>)

I.   **INTRODUCTION**---- (Short summary of the life of the Plaintiff)

II.   **LIABILITY**

A. FACTS---- (Straightforward recitation of the factual reasons Defendant is at fault and Plaintiff is without comparative fault; use answers to interrogatories, deposition testimony, diagrams, photos, and any helpful illustrations for the reader)

B. LAW--- (Set out succinctly the best legal arguments for your client's position citing relevant model jury instructions, statutes, cases)

III. DAMAGES

A. DIAGNOSED INJURIES---- (Synopsize the objective and provable injuries; use diagrams, medical illustrations, etc. to explain the injuries to the reader)

B. TREATMENT--- (Use time lines, charts, summaries of the past and future treatments, such as emergency treatment, hospitalizations, surgeries, physical therapies, home therapies, medical devices, etc.; again, any photos, drawings, etc. would be helpful to illustrate to the reader the serious nature and extent of the treatment, and its effect upon the Plaintiff and Plaintiff's life)

C. PERMANENCY--- (Any problem any treat/examining physician states is permanent should be recited and the effect on all Plaintiff ADL [96] activities of daily-living should be explained; as well as Plaintiff's life expectancy and "future risks" of surgery or worsening of the conditions)

D. PAST AND FUTURE ECONOMIC LOSS--- (Any past/future medical bills. Past/future lost income or loss of earning capacity, cost of substituted services, future life care. Itemize and/or estimate and justify any past and future out of pocket expenses.

E. SIGNIFICANT IMPACTS UPON THE PLAINTIFF'S LIFE--- (Explain in detail how Plaintiff's life has been permanently and significantly affected/changed; again, photos, exhibits, etc., showing "before and after" life of Plaintiff are helpful)

    F.   LIFE EXPECTANCY (S)---(If damages will continue for rest of clients/spouse/children's lives, then provide the up-to-date life expectancy)

IV.   **JURY VERDICT RESEARCH AND/OR SETTLEMENT DEMAND---** (With or without justification you may choose to make a settlement demand.... or not) (Include Judicial Interest)

CHAPTER EIGHT

DANGERS OF SETTLEMENT WITHOUT A LAWYER

The idea of settling a case without a lawyer often seems enticing and is often welcomed and encouraged by the insurance adjuster. However, *in all but a very few limited situations*, you are much better off hiring an attorney because a skilled attorney will probably get you several thousand, tens of thousands, hundreds of thousands, and even millions of dollars more than you can obtain by yourself.

In a minor injury case, one where you are fully recovered within the first 2-4 weeks, you may actually get more money in your pocket than you would if you hired a lawyer. However, if your injury last more than a month or you have significant economic loss, it is beneficial to contact a personal injury lawyer before any decisions are made as to the settlement of the claim. Additionally, when you realize you have a significant injury, whether it's based on how you feel or a medical opinion you received, you should not hesitate to hire a lawyer. This is true even if the accident is less than one day old.

For individuals that may choose to settle a large case of personal injury single-handedly, it is often to their detriment, as they often settle for compensation significantly below the fair value of their damages and injuries.

Liens/Subrogation/Right to Reimbursement

The following health Insurance providers may pay all or part of your medical bills following an accident, however, they all have liens, subrogation, and rights of reimbursement:

1. Medicaid

2. Medicare

3. ERISA-Government Plan

4. Tricare or other military plan

5. Government Employee Health Plan

6. Private Health Insurance such as Blue Cross Blue Shield

7. Health Care Providers with unpaid medical bills

If any of these are parties to your case, you SHOULD never settle your case while ignoring their rights. There can--and often will be-- significant repercussions. The best course of action if one of these is involved is to consult an attorney for assistance.

CHAPTER NINE

IDENTIFYING A GOOD LAWYER

In the event that you have realized that it's necessary to hire an attorney to handle your case, it is essential that you hire an experienced and qualified one.

The practice of law is large, and it is spread across various disciplines, including that of personal injury law. However, not many lawyers specialize in this field; though many may practice it. Therefore, it is important that you seek out a lawyer who devotes a significant amount of his/her time to personal injury litigation.

Education and Experience

In trying to determine if a lawyer is a a good lawyer, you can start by researching his/her educational background. The educational background will help you see how the lawyer got to where he is but it does little to nothing to show how effective the person is as a lawyer. The most significant practical experience occurs after law school. Law school teaches the lawyer the law, however, a lawyer doesn't fully learn how to apply it until he enters the real work and learns to apply it on a daily basis. Lawyers also attend CLE (continuing legal education) which provides practical experience. Additionally, you want to research the lawyer's trial experience. Although, most cases are settled prior to trial, an experienced trial attorney is often able to obtain a more significant settlement than one with little or no trial experience.

Most lawyers and firms have a website that contains information on their practice areas as well as some of their prior case results. This is a good starting point to research a lawyer, but it should not be your only research.

Lawyer Websites and Beyond

Lawyer websites also usually contain sales ads or pitches that provide no substantive value. These include the following:

- No fee, No recovery
  - Personal injury lawyers use contingency fees; which mean the lawyer only gets paid at the end of the case. This is true for virtually every personal injury lawyer
- Aggressive
  - This statement should be verified by looking beyond the lawyer's website
- Free initial consultation
  - I have never seen or heard of a personal injury lawyer charging a consult fee.

- Millions recovered

  - This statement can be misleading in several ways. For example, if 100 cases are settled for $10,000 each that's a million but it does nothing to prove that fair settlement values were reached. Alternatively, if there are 10 lawyers in a firm that settle $100,000 each per year, that also does nothing to add value to this statement.

  - The lawyer should be able to discuss a few cases where the value was significantly more than what the client anticipated.

  - It's ok to ask the lawyer about these in person or on the phone because they may not always be on the website if the settlements were confidential.

- 100+ years of combined experience

- This is just math. The law firm simply adds up the number of years of all the lawyers in the firm. Many of those lawyers may have little to no experience in personal injury law.

Actions Speak Louder than Words

In deciding on a lawyer, you should also beware of:

1. A lawyer promising a certain outcome or dollar amount

    a. There is no way for a lawyer to definitively tell you at the outset, the amount of money he will get you if you hire him. Additionally, this practice is prohibited by Louisiana's lawyer ethics rules.

2. A Lawyer with Negative Public Image

    a. If there's a lot of negativity surrounding the lawyer's reputation or past results, the insurance company is probably aware of it also. The lawyer's reputation is one factor considered by insurance companies when making settlement offers.

It is important to consider and contact as many as 3-5 law firms until you find someone you are comfortable with.

You should also ask friends, family members, church members, and co-workers to give you the name of lawyers they have had a good experience with or the name of someone they can call who's had good experiences with a lawyer.

Furthermore, some sites can be visited in helping choose a lawyer as they represent an accurate and independent assessment of a lawyer's background and collective clients' experiences. Examples of such independent sites are AVVO.com. google reviews, Super Lawyers, Top 100 Trial Lawyers, and Best Lawyers in America. The right lawyer for your case may not have a footprint on all these sites, however, he/she should be on at least one. DO not rely solely on reviews on the lawyer's website because the lawyer decides what's on his website.

ASK THE RIGHT QUESTIONS

- How many years have you been practicing personal injury law?

- Have you handled cases similar to mine?

- What do you think will be the hardest part of my case?

- What is the procedure for handling my case?

- Who in your office will be working on my case and what will each person's job be?

- How do you intend to keep me informed?

- Can I get a copy of the fee agreement?
  - A lawyer should never pressure you to sign a fee agreement. You should be

given an opportunity to review and
think the agreement over if you are
unsure about

CHAPTER TEN

CAN WE ASSIST YOUR CASE?

Certain factors are considered in determining our decision on whether to render assistance or not; thus, these factors are discussed below. These are not our opinions on whether or not you actually have a legitimate claim but rather these are our office policies on cases we elect to get involved in. Any of the following situations are cases we are highly likely to accept, however, we will consult with you on any cases even if it isn't a perfect fit for our criteria:

1. Medical Bills and Lost Wages
   a. If you have or anticipate suffering any of these following an accident.

2. Property damage to your car of $1,000.00 or more

   a. Sometimes, significant injuries result from property damage less than this amount so don't let the amount of damage to your car deter you from contacting a lawyer if you have significant medical issues.

3. You were NOT at fault

   a. Unfortunately, if the accident was your fault, we cannot help you.

4. Medical treatment

   a. If you have had or anticipate medical treatment beyond 1-2 visits

5. Accident happened within the last 10 months.

   a. If you are involved in an accident you have one year to file a lawsuit. The 10 month cut-off gives us sufficient time to investigate and file the lawsuit on your behalf. Please do not wait until the last minute to contact a lawyer.

CHAPTER ELEVEN

<u>CASES WE DO NOT</u>

ACCEPT

We have given the criteria for cases we accept; therefore, it is only reasonable that we provide criteria for cases that we do not accept. This does not mean that other firms would decline the case; it simply refers to cases we have chosen to decline.

We do not accept cases with multiple prior claims. When a person has multiple prior claims with injuries to the same body part or parts it's almost impossible to resolve the case for a fair amount. Additionally, judges and jurors are very suspicious of these sorts of cases and routinely decide against the plaintiff.

Also, we do not accept cases where another lawyer or law firm has been involved for a substantial period of time, especially if they have already filed a lawsuit. It's acceptable to switch lawyers early on, however, once a lawyer has devoted significant time and resources, he will have a significant lien or interest in your case for the work done. The client has the option to switch lawyers at any time, however, we rarely accept these cases for the reasons stated above, and routinely advise against such behavior absent significant ethical violations by the current lawyer.

CHAPTER TWELVE

Filing the Lawsuit

In Louisiana you have one year from the date of the accident to file a lawsuit. I do not recommend filing a personal injury case without the assistance of a lawyer. The technical expertise required to properly handle a case, other than a very minor case, requires years of legal training and experience. Drafting and filing a lawsuit requires a profound understanding of legal concepts such as jurisdiction, venue, liability, causation, damages, evidence rules and the rules of court. The moment you realize your injuries are significant and your case is not likely to be settled you should consult and hire a lawyer so that he/she may begin working on it.

CONCLUSION

Through this book, I have attempted to provide guidance on resolving a personal injury case without the assistance of a lawyer, as well as warnings on when to call a lawyer and the dangers of resolving your case without a lawyer.

This book does not replace the need to consult a lawyer when the complex issues discussed herein arise, as it's impossible to write a book that can cover every possible scenario in such a complex arena.

www.ingramcontent.com/pod-product-compliance
Lightning Source LLC
Chambersburg PA
CBHW030529220526
45463CB00007B/2763